ASCENSION

ASCENSION

LUIVETTE RESTO

POEMS

TIA CHUCHA PRESS
LOS ANGELES

Printed in the United States.

ISBN 978-1-882688-45-6

Book Design: Jane Brunette
Cover painting by Ernesto Yerena Montejano. Used with permission.
Back cover photo: Jay Ho

Some of these poems first appeared in the following publications:

Palabra: A Magazine of Chicano & Latino Literary: "Plátano Maduro Dreams"
Kweli Journal: "Perfect Attendance"
TYCA Poetry Month Celebration: "No More Tacos in Gwinettt County"
Writers at Work Poet of the Month: "No More Tacos in Gwinettt County"
Our Spirit, Our Reality!: Sowing the Seeds Anthology: "Incubus," "Medical History,"
     "Fortunate Failures"
Oranges and Sardines: "Sonnet for Our Lexicon"
The Mas Tequila Review: "Sweathshop Tiffany's," "Scars," "Thank You Ricky Martín"
Poetry Superhighway: Poem of the Week, "Ascension"
Hinchas de Poesia: "No More Tacos in Gwinnett County," "Ascension," "Your Mom's Jesus"
Ginosko Literary Journal: "Skyline"
Poetic Diversity: "Skyline"

PUBLISHED BY:
Tía Chucha Press
A Project of Tía Chucha's Centro Cultural, Inc.
PO Box 328
San Fernando, CA 91341
www.tiachucha.com

DISTRIBUTED BY:
Northwestern University Press
Chicago Distribution Center
11030 South Langley Avenue
Chicago IL 60628

Tia Chucha Press is the publishing wing of Tia Chucha's Centro Cultural, Inc., a 501 (c) 3 non-profit corporation. Tia Chucha's Centro Cultural has received funding for this book from the National Endowment for the Arts and individual donors. Other funding for Tia Chucha's Centro Cultural's programming and operations has come from the California Arts Council, Los Angeles County Arts Commission, Los Angeles Department of Cultural Affairs, The California Community Foundation, the Annenberg Foundation, the Weingart Foundation, National Association of Latino Arts and Culture, Ford Foundation, MetLife, Southwest Airlines, the Andy Warhol Foundation for the Visual Arts, the Thrill Hill Foundation, the Middleton Foundation, Center for Cultural Innovation, John Irvine Foundation, Not Just Us Foundation, the Attias Family Foundation, and the Guacamole Fund, among others. Donations have also come from Bruce Springsteen, John Densmore of The Doors, Jackson Browne, Lou Adler, Richard Foos, Gary Stewart, Charles Wright, Adrienne Rich, Tom Hayden, Dave Marsh, Jack Kornfield, Jesus Trevino, David Sandoval, Denise Chávez and John Randall of the Border Book Festival, Luis & Trini Rodríguez, and many more.

TABLE OF CONTENTS

Skyline / 9

Ascension / 10

Logophile / 11

Leave it to the Weatherman / 12

Incubus / 13

The Superlative of Sex / 14

Surrender / 15

Dedications / 16

Your Mom's Jesus / 17

Pink Balloons / 18

Uncoordinated / 19

Ampersand / 20

Constellations / 21

Confessions of a Love Poem / 22

Sonnet for Our Lexicon / 23

On the Rooftop / 24

Circle Any That Apply / 27

Ganas / 28

A Poem for Me / 29

Mujer Maravillosa / 31

Some Days / 33

Aubade of the Grouchy Dancing Bear / 34

Fortunate Failures / 35

Medical History / 37

The Pendeja Syndrome / 38

Unapologetic / 40

Latina Etymology / 41

Kindergarten Translations / 43

Sweatshop Tiffany's / 44

Christmas Lies / 46

A Poem for My Misogynist Colleague / 48

No More Tacos in Gwinnett County / 50

A Poem for the Students of UCSD / 51

Perfect Attendance / 52

Plátano Maduro Dreams / 54

Statistic / 56

Ode to Doorknockers / 57

Yes / 58

Palms Up / 59

The Poet's Bomba / 60

Hail María / 61

Pedro's Bodega / 62

Thank You Ricky Martín / 64

Letters to a Young Latina Poet / 66

For
my revolutionaries

SKYLINE

She didn't kiss me like you.
That's what you said
as we sat on my bedroom fire escape,
staring at the luminescent red and green lights
of the Empire State Building.

Christmas was almost here.
Our third one if I counted correctly.

We never faced one another
as you spoke to a starless night sky
and I listened to taxis curse at brave pedestrians.

You didn't love me the same way anymore.
You needed to find yourself
before you could give to others.
I wasn't what you needed right now.
You didn't see a future or a family with me.

I didn't cry.
Not for your satisfaction
but for mine.
I didn't want to remember myself that way.

Thoughtfully the city exhaled
a wind full of flurries up my thin nightshirt.
Shuttering for the first time,
I got up and dusted the rust off my jeans.

ASCENSION

We lay on the hood of your '96 Tercel
watching the planes land underneath
an unusually clear L.A. sky,

imagining heading off to lands
where money is abundant
like sand and possibilities.

And when "Love Song" by The Cure played on the radio,
you dragged the tops of your fingernails
up and down my forearm,

as we shared the same early memories of
smoking bidis for the first time
in your step-mom's basement,
watching 1970s porn like it was a documentary,
reciting each other's fortunes from our Chinese takeout.

Logic dictated that you wouldn't like me,
allow me to touch the scar on your right eyebrow
and ask for its story.
But you did.

You confessed to enjoying the silence of
libraries, funeral homes, churches.
Became an atheist when your parents divorced,
left you wondering if you would ever be a good father.

Feeling the coldness of metal on my back
I inched closer to your side of the car,
listened to the unevenness of your breath
between the sounds of jet engines.

LOGOPHILE

You like the way my lips
come together when I say the word
serendipity.

Something about the letter p
coming together just to be pulled
apart again to complete the word.

What about post meridiem?
Begins together,
ends together.

Doesn't count.
It's two words.
You mumbled
under the goose feather comforter.

Corruption is better.
The tongue has a bit of a solo
before acquiescing.

The morning sunshine
intruded our conversation
and barren apartment walls
as candle wax trickled over
wine bottlenecks.

LEAVE IT TO THE WEATHERMEN

to make predictions of tomorrow
with talks of jet streams and
minus ten wind chill factors
bringing me back to our first nor'easter
stranded on the right shoulder of I95,
your index finger calmly swirling her initials
on the passenger's side window.

Leave me with the memory of
an aurora borealis sending yellow
and green ribbons across the Manitoba sky
when I recognized who I needed to be
and who you never were.

INCUBUS

I lied when I said I love you in the rain,
my selfish cinematic fantasy
for a three dimensional romantic comedy.
I didn't apologize for making you believe
in the alleged validity of my words.

But you didn't let me get off easy.
You became my incubus.
Haunting my dreams at night
with candlelight dinners on New York City rooftops,
serenades below a Shakespearean balcony,
slow dances underneath a Mediterranean half-moon.

I tried to exorcise you from our nightly excursions,
rejected your existence,
your feelings,
my feelings,
like I did before.
I was cruel, vindictive, merciless.

But your fingers hushed my nonsensical lips
letting me believe in the validity of you.

THE SUPERLATIVE OF SEX

Using my tongue,
I play connect the dots
with the freckles and beauty marks on your chest.
The wetness of our bodies in my shower
clash like the acoustic echo of lightening.

Your right hand massages the tips of my earlobe,
tugging at the flesh like silly putty,
while the left hand glides strands of hair off my face.

Our eyes explore the possibilities of our bodies
as blue violas on my nightstand wilt in the sunlight.

SURRENDER

You were sexier than
a trumpet solo
in a salsa song.
Why would anyone
say no.

DEDICATIONS

He wrote songs
under broken street lamps,
long bike rides along Pacific Coast Highway horizons,
hot sauce stained napkins from his favorite diner,
on his arm when paper was absent
and inspiration cataclysmic
like the epicenter of desert earthquakes.

Found music
in the saltiness of a scorned woman,
the gentleness of a child's first step,
in the inexplicable tears of unilateral love.

The longitude and latitude
of his verses and baritone voice,
recreated the nervous excitement
of impending thunder
after lightening strikes.

He never knew my name,
or the caress of my hand
each time he said,
"This one goes out to…"

YOUR MOM'S JESUS

was his retort
when he felt
the impending loss of an argument
about arbitrary line breaks,
emphatic punctuation marks like the dash,
fantasy football team draft picks.

Where is the Messiah
when his father cannot silence
the symphony of aerial bombs
over Korea and Vietnam.

Where was Jesus
when his mother had breast cancer,
plaguing his middle school years
with nightmares of zombies
feasting on his mother's carcass.

He developed road rage
counting all of the Jesus fish
plastered on the back of cars, trucks
and once a tractor.

Weekly, he'd yank the metal Ichthys off cars
at mall parking structures,
bewildering Sunday school teachers
and catechism children.

Agnostic became his permanent status update,
highlighted on his dating profile,
tattooed over his heart in his mother's handwriting.

PINK BALLOONS

With only a bounty of pink and purple,
existing against his collage of darkness,
she plucked from her helium bouquet
a solitary soft pink balloon,
as the Atlantic Ocean applauded
the random act of kindness
witnessed on its boardwalk,
once saturated with $5 women,
peddlers, and morally questionable
business men.

Sea gulls wondered
if the boy will remember the lace
at the bottom of the girl's dress or
the black bow buckle of her patent leather shoes,
will she remember the coldness of his fingertips or
the silhouette of his sullen face
as the sun set on both of them.

UNCOORDINATED

The jukebox was out of order
so you hummed your favorite song.
Motioned me to the dance floor
where I politely informed you
that I couldn't dance without looking
like my dad when Rod Stewart comes on.
My only contribution was my head
nodding to the beat
while my arms and feet tried
catching up with the rest of me.

In my fantasies
I am a graceful dancer,
minus the pink itchy tutu,
worthy of Alvin Ailey's
and Bob Fosse's praise.
Propelled on men's shoulders,
swiveling down their torsos
like the last bit of raindrops from a palm leaf.
My hands perfectly stretched to the sky.
Followed by the standing ovations,
encores, and gardenias thrown
on the stage.

You didn't laugh at me,
my feet, my wannabe ballerina daydreams,
or the way I had to stop and clap
to find the rhythms of sound
swimming in your mouth.

Instead you grabbed my hand,
turned my body towards your warmth,
absent of judgment.

AMPERSAND

Like the 27th letter of the alphabet
he was forgotten.
The way his thumb caressed her hand
when ferris wheels made her anxious,
twirled her in an embrace
as she carefully flipped blueberry pancakes.

He was misunderstood and misinterpreted
so she renamed him Mondegreen
for those private moments,
sitting in the solarium,
betting one another to see which rain drop
tumbled faster on the plated glass windows.

CONSTELLATIONS

Adding dizzying color
like a kaleidoscope
to his inertia,
he gravitated towards her.
As she asked to be part
of his constellation of paramours
and unfinished paintings.

Liberating one another
like a Cardenal poem.

CONFESSIONS OF A LOVE POEM

Along the coast of Isla Negra.
my affairs remain buried.

I wanted companionship so I became a couplet
given to the whims of haughty men.

They never stopped being haughty and I never could
so I became my own elegy,

with superfluous stanzas about unrequited love
and the cruelties of my lusts.

In the chrysalis of words,
I became sonnet one hundred and one.

Immortalized in the epitome of reciprocal affection.

SONNET FOR OUR LEXICON

The first morning we spoke the language of our ancestors
confusion spread between us like an epidemic.
Your furrowed brow stripped my language naked
as I asked you to leave the room but you stood your ground.
I repeated in my Boricua Spanish to come back later,
but your Chicano ears understood right now.

You questioned the validity of the word *safacón*,
laughed when I pointed to the barrette in my hair
    and called it a *pinche*,
I insisted an orange is a *china* not a *naranja*,
how *guagua* sounded much better than *autobús*.

As we compiled a list of our lexicons,
"Mi Viejo San Juan" began to play in the background.
Your hand asked for a dance
and my body said *Simón*.

ON THE ROOFTOP

PART I

Overlooking the Webster Avenue exit,
we talked about distant galaxies,
the inevitable takeover of extraterrestrials.

They wouldn't be like E.T., green, or bug-eyed
you said as a toothpick slid from one
corner of your mouth to the other.
Our aliens would be the epitome of cool
with a swagger no one had ever seen.
No shiny silver uniforms for them or
some stupid monogrammed letter on their chest.
No uniforms period.
Just a Downy smelling t-shirt and jeans.

What about intelligence?
Letting the nicotine take over my lungs.

Oh they'll be smart.
No more of this you must live over here,
you can't do this bullshit.
Negative words do not exist in distant galaxies.
They know how to live out there.

Screeching tires from a car ready to run the red
shifted our eyes towards the concrete,
smell of burnt Goodyear tires,
and a litany of Spanish curses.

Yeah, they know how to live out there,
as you spat the toothpick out your mouth
into the cloudless sky.

Part II

The October wind waffs
the stench of new tar patches.
Sulfur rushes into my nostrils,
pouring the last drop of an '02 Cab.

I toast to our move-in day.
The Thanksgiving we attempted to cook a turkey
only to end up here with a bucket of chicken
and a six-pack of Coronas.

I drink to my idiocies.
Believing in late night meetings,
playing Scrabble with a virtual stranger,
pasting vacation pictures in scrapbooks,
recreating an impossible
out of an aging relationship.

Lucky are the make believe children.
Never witnesses to the countless
police visits, broken picture frames.
Frail like tissue paper.

Part III

Mid-afternoon between Transformers and He-Man
Angel watched two men across the street
put a gun to the back of Don Hector's head.
He was probably on his way to C-Town or
taking his doctor's orders walk around the block.

Angel opened his mouth to scream the latest expletive
he learned on St. Theresa's schoolyard.
Motherfuckers sounded right in this situation.
But silence joined the stillness of the humid afternoon
as his mouth remained frozen in an O.

The old man didn't fight back.
He knelt like he does every Sunday.
Praying to hit the lotto, his wife's spirit,
a day without taking so many pills.

He never turned around
as they searched his pockets,
running away with $27 dollars in food stamps
and a faded wedding picture.

Angel finally closed his mouth with a sigh
as he watched Don Hector pick himself up
dust off his knees, and walk home.

CIRCLE ANY THAT APPLY

ignited like the sparks on my uncle's match,
afraid of being alone next birthday,
motherless before hitting puberty,
always a step-son never anyone's son,
the fruition of my parents' dreams,
sex in a pantsuit and glasses, wannabe breakdancer,
profound idiot, prisoner of technology, cautiously optimistic,
closet reality tv show watcher, highest scorer in donkey Kong,
perennial procrastinator, melanin carrier, fallible, memorable like
blood stains on a sidewalk, refreshing like rain on spring grass,
dutiful child, catalyst of a melee, tears on a shirt,
intellectual of useless facts, cynical, reliable like a church pew,
hopeful when a shooting star falls from the sky,
the best interpretative dancer to "Single Ladies,"
insecure decision maker, second guesser, insular,
conservative about taxes, liberal with others' money,
inventor of geek chic, seeker of truth in a pile of lies,
vulnerable like fir trees during Christmas time.

GANAS

He painted my portrait
before we met,
as if his brushes
knew me from another life
where I led revolutions with a machete
instead of a pen and a saucy look.

A POEM FOR ME

begins from a selfish place
with secret wants of finding a home
on someone's bookshelf,
reiterated from someone's lips,
engrained in someone's memory.
This poem is for me
not for the masses.
Meter, forms, line breaks
do   not
concern
me, so I say

forget the critics
who may or may not,
dissect my stanzas,
determining my similes and metaphors
pedestrian or exquisite like Tahitian pearls.

I write this poem
to remind me of
the prolonging solitude of darkness.
My long list of defense mechanisms,
crafting moats and stonewalls,
impenetrable like the nature of God.

This poem is
independent, vulnerable,
chicken shit, wishes it could play the piano,
awkward meeting new people, caustically truthful, sardonic,
unnaturally nurturing, generous with smiles,
disgustingly loyal, morose,
uncomfortable with compliments.

This poem is for me

a reminder to be
my own muse,
when pages yellow and delicately fold
like forgotten calla lilies on kitchen tables.

MUJER MARAVILLOSA

Staring at her Wonder Woman tattoo
sipping her café Bustelo,
puro negro like Abuelito,
Valentina begins her annual fantasy about her funeral.

Would her absentee father
cry a single tear on his left cheek
where they share the same birthmark.
Would he speak fondly about fictional conversations
about Fathers's Days and birthdays.

She imagined her mother still like Venus,
with condolences floating at her like
Monarch butterflies over Michoacán.

The deaths were always
noble and brave.
Breast cancer
liker her Tía Songa
who made three children instant orphans.

Sometimes it wasn't cancer.
Other days Valentina overdosed on
men and their compliments
ugly, pelo malo, gordita.

Sleeping pills would be peaceful.
Lie beautiful, naked and pitied like Norma Jean,
but drowning sounded wet and sexy.

Her pulsating veins taunted her mornings
but she was too squeamish.
She didn't want to be like her friend
who left a very confused five-year-old girl
behind with a lifetime of questions and doubts.

Unlike her friends
Valentina had no desire for children.
Sex was an option to be enjoyed
not a vehicle for procreation.

Children were not a definition of her worth.
She was priceless like Cortez's gold,
Seated Woman, or *Moonlight Sonata*.

She would be eulogized at Ortiz Funeral Home,
friends will cry about
her generosity and good spirit.
Forget calling her
backstabber or bochinchosa.
Forgive her for her brutal honesty, hogging all of the french fries,
never paying them back the $20 she borrowed in 1998.

She will be buried with Miles Davis CDs,
unmailed love letters to all of her "shoulda, coulda been"
boyfriends,
a pocket size Bible the corner street fanatic doled out
    during the holidays,
blank sheets of paper for posthumous poems,
three Cala Lily petals, tokens from the 6 train,
sand from Orchard Beach, and
her first edition of *Puerto Rican Obituary*.

Savoring the last tastes
Valentina tries counting
the overlap of coffee rings on the table.

SOME DAYS

Mirrors should be called
imperfection enhancers
as her grandfather's nose
stares back at her.

She never knew him really
even though they shared the same facial feature,
bad temper, and hatred for beets.

Introduced her to the beauty of "Bohemian Rhapsody,"
pulled down her corkscrew curls and
acted surprise when they bounced back
to their original shape.

She thinks about the desecration of her grandfather's sarcophagus,
Can she will him back if she closes her eyes tight
like the white patent leathered shoes she wore on Easter Sundays.

Dreaming in blue
as the neverending homily echoed off marble pillars,
erasing the congregation's public sins
of all the "goddamnits" and "Jesus fucking Christs."
No one confessed about the make out sessions
between the altar boys and choir girls
behind the St. Christopher statue.
The donation basket financing
Rev. Bill's Caddie.

"Baby girl, remember some sinners don't wake up early on Sundays,"
as your index finger and thumb,
dry and ashy from those masonry years,
raise the volume slowly to *Birth of the Cool*.

AUBADE OF THE GROUCHY DANCING BEAR

She tells me not to disturb her as she slumbers.
Her word. Not mine.
To her slumber is what grouchy bears like her do.

Sleep is for women who shake their hair,
laugh carefully in public, think twice before speaking,
never second guess or interrupt.

Slumber is for women who chop off their hair
and donate it to children who get tired of combing
Barbie's synthetic yellow strands.

women who laugh hearty like sailors,
possibly chortle at the end of a very offensive,
unchristian, feminist card retraction kind of joke.
Slumber is for women who dance
in front of department store mirrors
with no music anywhere near.

for women who punctuate
sentences with a buffet of four letter words,
obscene hand gestures or raised eyebrows.

Slumber is for women with percolating opinions,
never nervous of rebuttals, confident in her resolve,
categorizes her socks into happy and sad piles.

Slumber is for grouchy bears who buy first editions,
learn the first bars of "Clair de Lune,"
stand in line for midnight showings,

remember not only birthdays but
the anniversary of scars and broken bones.

FORTUNATE FAILURES

February 2000

The blade never touched the skin,
the window never opened,
the pills never swallowed.

I threw my purple plastic rosary
on your Bacardi stained carpet
where we shared many kisses,

toasting to our potential new life and
future revolutionary children
who would take over the world with
their brown berets and propagandas of peace.

I damned God for my tears,
my obstacles, my family,
for Father Flynn making me believe in the mysterious ways
of the Lord and the divinity of an alleged master plan.

I looked in the mirror to see
the redness of my eyes,
the swell of my face,
the moisture on my forehead,
the flare of my nostrils,
the rise and fall of my chest.

Sadness seemed so inviting
in the vacancy of options.

I imagined our children
asking why momma was crying
in the middle of the afternoon.
You explaining to them

why momma needed those white pills in the morning.

I imagined your arms wrapped around me
telling me you loved us.

MEDICAL HISTORY

As the doctor rattled off
all the expectations for month number five,
the relief nurse began her
gauntlet of routine questions.

Allergies: Penicillin.
Surgeries: Lump removed from right breast.
Previous medications: Zoloft.
First pregnancy: No.
Miscarriage: No.
Termination: Yes.

It was the fifth time
I said yes.

Became a slut,
murderer, mother.

The fifth time I left the doctor's office asking for forgiveness,
blamed my husband for being a lousy boyfriend,
felt the sting of Novocain injected into my cervix,
held back tears when I saw a two-year-old
knowing that's how old you would be,
remembered your heart was still beating that day.

My repeated yeses
became the Hail Marys
I never said to you.

THE PENDEJA SYNDROME

has claimed many victims.
Symptoms may include

Waiting for his phone call but tell yourself
that you don't care either way.

Replaying his message fifty two times
analyzing the tone each time.

Bumping into him and his new fiancée
at the open bar wearing your

"wish-you-could-have-this-back-don't-you" dress.
Meeting him at Washington Square Park

for a 3 a.m. rendezvous as you look at your watch
and the winos every five minutes.

Really believing him and his ex are just friends.
Giving your body before your heart.

Envisioning a future when you say "I love you"
and he responds "I'm flattered."

Excusing him when he calls you stupid in public,
holding onto the belief that you can change him.

Shuttering at the idea of an entering an empty house.
Letting him put it in for two minutes,

if not they really do turn blue.
Writing your name and his last name

just to see what they would like together.
Swallow when you really want to spit.

Presume it does happen to all men
and give him one more try.

Give him a key to your apartment
only to smell a different perfume on your pillow.

Pretending he is the one because you are tired
of being the CEO and client of the spinsters for life club.
Repeat to yourself he only does it because he loves you
while you wear long sleeves in July.

See him laugh with another
as he swears it means nothing and

you mean everything.

UNAPOLOGETIC

for my comadres

I will not make up excuses
like a baseball player
for ordering a second bottle of wine
or burping after drinking a Malta,
I will not hesitate
telling the nosey woman at Target,
to shut her unsolicited wannabe
CPS parenting advice,

I will not say an extra set of Hail Mary's
for giving the middle finger
to the blue haired old lady at Costco
for taking my parking space,
I will not apologize
like a politician for
calling you an insensitive asshole
after breaking up with me via text,

I will not stop nor regret
documenting my victories,
flaws, missteps, and charms
to soothe your insecurities,

and I will not beg for pardon
like an Evangelical preacher
for biting your lip in the morning,
making you have good reason
for calling in sick.

LATINA ETYMOLOGY

According to Puerto Rican folklore
my name would have been Luis Omar
if I was born a boy.

I was created out of spontaneity
not stupidity or love.

Like my conception
my name was created via mindless thoughts
crashing into one another.

My grandmother
the neologist,
stumbled upon my name
doodling on her desk pad
the permutations of my parents' names.

Growing up
I cursed when teachers could not pronounce it on first days,
cringed when strangers asked if I was part French,
watched Romper Room every morning
hoping Miss Molly would say my name
when she looked in the magic mirror,
idolized the Marías and Socorros of the world
because accents and double r's never hovered over my head.

Resentment grew like weeds
as my name was confused for others:
Louisa, Lizette, Lucretia.

Nicknames were an option
but I didn't want to be called Vet or Corvette
to satisfy lazy, Anglofied tongues.

Masculine pseudonyms prevailed
stripping me of my curves and vulnerability every time
I heard Lou or Louie.

Sometimes I fantasized my name in lights
but my illusions quickly dimmed like the twilight.
Because accolades were only bestowed upon sonorous names like
Megan, Vanessa, and Kate.
While dissident names became the
poet laureates of the Goya aisle.

Maturity eventually settled
and accents never provided shade
like Peking willows.

Staring at my reflection,
I find the common denominators in my name.

One half
an absent father who willingly never saw his only child grow up.
One half
an alcoholic mother who refused to see her only child grow up.

I was created out of spontaneity
not stupidity or love.

KINDERGARTEN TRANSLATIONS

1982 brought a plethora of newness:
Winter on my island skin, earmuffs drowning out
Spanish conversations doubting why we moved,
snowflakes on my tongue as I ran to catch the #42 bus,
sirens instead of coquís at night.

The classroom covered in UPS brown,
bulletin boards decorated in primary colors,
the smell of tacky glue and fingerpaint lingered in the air
as my size 8 shoe stepped on the checkered floor.

Mrs. Farrell made me her an impromptu show n' tell
introducing me to twenty-eight confused faces, wooden easels, and
the alphabet wrapping the room like a birthday present.
The "ch" sadly absent from the wall.

The back of the class became my new hideaway
right behind Vanessa Vives
who unknowingly became my best friend
as she translated Mrs. Farrell's lesson about the seasons.

A colorful chalk drawn tree on the blackboard stared back at me
the orange and red leaves resembling the rows of mango trees
I left behind.

Mrs. Farrell asked the class
what happens to the leaves in autumn.
The trees wiggles them off and they fall on its roots.
Vanessa answered for me.

SWEATSHOP TIFFANY'S

Summer 1996

In the summer of 1996,
Don Luis offered me my first paying job:
8 cents per button I latched onto
a turquoise velvet bag,
10 cents if I could hook
the matching drawstring through the holes.

My work station shared by a young, voluptuous señorita.
A scorching glue gun her only weapon
against Don Luis's roaming hands.

In a room the size of my Bronx basement,
older women and their sewing machines
sang along to Marc Anthony ballads,
10 foot fans in place of air conditioning
whirred in response with the chorus,
"y hubo alguien."

And they were somebody.
Mothers, grandmothers, aunts, daughters,
immigrants without the documentation but
with the heart and understanding of capitalism
like a true Americano.
They got paid more than I:
14 cents per sewn garment.

Everything under the table
including the half hour homemade lunches
eaten in a storage room substituting as a cafeteria
mixed with the smells of sweat, exploitation, and arroz con pollo.

Ten years later I entered into my first Tiffany's
filled with smiles on women's faces, empty pockets of remorseful
husbands,
commission quotas being met, surprise engagements.

As I touched a velvet turquoise bag,
the cash registers sang
y hubo alguien.

CHRISTMAS LIES

Yes, I was an Obama Mama.
Decorated my car with kitschy bumper stickers.
Bought an Obama is My Homeboy t-shirt.
Believed in hope.
Change.
Hope for change.
Change in hope.
Heard "He Got Game" by Public Enemy
when I saw his numbers.
Cold called voters
and reminded them that
no he isn't a Muslim,
yes he is an American,
and yes he believes in God.

Stared at the TV screen
with glassy eyes
when he greeted a Chicago crowd
a third dimensional revised version of the American dream.
My six-year-old son asked
why did this man made me cry,
who was he?
And when I replied,
he's our president.
My son instantly said
he wanted to be that some day,
wear bright ties with dark suits,
wave flags, smile broadly at crowds.

"Yes you can, Antonio."
I said in the best imitation of
our new leader.
This time I didn't feel I was mommy lying

like I do around Christmas time
and pretend to leave Santa voicemail messages
about Antonio's latest good deeds and timeouts.
This time I knew his statement
could be a future truth
along with his quest to be an astronaut,
paleontologist, or a ninja.

But the euphoria of Election Day
and ubiquitous discussions of post-racial America
dissipated like confetti when the economy
didn't bounce back after Inauguration Day,
a Puerto Rican woman was chastised for making a wise crack,
an American's health reduced to a business plan,
Christian churches celebrated the paradox of holy book burning,
American states demanded fellow Americans
    prove their citizenship.

All of it making it feel like Christmas.

A POEM FOR MY MISOGYNIST COLLEAGUE

Your keen observation skills were in full force
in the teacher's lounge when you stated
the reason why I may get a new course approved
"Oh, it's because you are a woman that they
listen to you instead of me."

Yes Captain Obvious my extra X chromosome
doubles as a secret weapon of persuasion,
luring the Mobil guy to give me an extra squeeze of gas,
the pimply teenager at McDonalds to throw a few extra fries
    in my bag,
maintain the attention of a lackluster classroom
the day we discuss the eleven uses of a comma.

It must be the way I flip my hair when I say my name,
the new shade of eye shadow the MAC counter guy
told me would bring out the dark brown in my eyes
and make me look just absolutely fabulous
in a pant suit or a mini-skirt.
No it must be how I laugh at men's jokes even though
they make no sense and fall flatter than my chest
    in elementary school.
Speaking of breasts, it could be the power of the twins
in this pushup bra making me forget
the permanent gravitational effects of nursing
or it could be my flawless body courtesy to the invention of Spanx.
Maybe it's my inherited long legs making it always impossible
    to find pants
without having me look like a flood survivor.
Or is it the way I eat a banana, burrito, hot dog.

It cannot be my intelligence, hard work,
writing skills, ability to talk to people
without making them feel less than,

listen to the subtleties of a student's story
hidden between run-on sentences.

It cannot be because you are a
self-righteous, arrogant, asshole
who has the ability to clear a room in .6 seconds
the minute you open your mouth with an unsolicited opinion,
have students give up trying because they don't
regurgitate your ideas in a debate.

No. It must be my superpowers.

NO MORE TACOS IN GWINNETT COUNTY

July 2006

When the last brown footsteps
walked out of Garfield High School
for the second time,
Gwinnett County, Georgia, declared
death to the taco stand.

No more dollar corn tortillas
satiating the appetites of
housekeepers, gardeners, waiters,
peach pickers, janitors, nannies.
Giving them all a five-minute taste of Juarez.

The tacos migrated to Philadelphia with hopes
of finding a friendlier and hungrier crowd.
Instead they found picket lines with
Philly cheesesteaks holding signs.

A sub owner had followed Georgia with a sign of his own
"This is America. When ordering, speak English."
In the kitchen, Manuel and Juan
diced peppers and onions in silence.

Paranoia and sign making spread to the Midwest
where a Butler County, Ohio, jail
had a sign pointed to it
"Illegal Aliens Here."

The steel bars shivered
because hunger for
revolution and absolution
only existed here.

A POEM FOR THE STUDENTS OF UCSD

With the click of a mouse,
viral invitations honoring Black History Month
titled The Compton Cookout
spread like locusts on cultivated crops.
A call for girls with bad attitudes and poor clothing,
guys with gold teeth and broken English,
fried chicken and watermelon on the menu.

Post-Obama speeches of progress faded
as humor and first amendment rights
substituted for human decency and backwards thinking.
Despite Brown vs. Board of Education, Mendez vs. Westminster,
a noose hung outside the library.
Despite King, Chavez, Parks, Farmer, Huerta,
the word nigger and wetback decorated university walls like it
was 1964.
Despite the news headlines and recycled administrative rhetoric,
the words student and activist were synonymous once again because
another university is possible.

PERFECT ATTENDANCE

Like Grecian statues
they sit quietly on the first day
waiting intentionally for the
acknowledgment of existence.

Andrew the ex-high school running back,
where his A's equated to touchdowns.
The field his temporary escape
from friends turned gang members,
college his final escape
from the irony of his city,
El Monte.

Guadalupe works two jobs part-time,
hits the books part-time,
supports her family full-time,
tries to save for her white wedding
as another problem set finds a solution,
her potential brighter than a meteor shower
off Saturn's E ring.

Eun arrived not too long to America
F.O.B. her more sophisticated Asian-American
classmates call her,
she takes many notes but
never raises her voice,
contemplates changing her name to Ellen
for the convenience of her American teacher's tongue.

Deepak and his pugree
receive the suspicious eye on first days and
if the president announces the day orange,
he has the lunch table all to himself.
No one knows about his snowboarding trophies,
love for a Dodger dog or pristine collection of Jordans.

Laura, ex-con, mother, sponsor,
the classroom her first place
after twenty years of concrete and steel.
Her right thumb and forefinger,
with a shooting star tattooed between it,
turns grammar book pages judiciously.

Linda,
pregnant at 16,
married at 18,
divorced at 28,
old enough to be a grandmother six times,
born before the freeways dissected East LA
into two halves of poverty.

David back from Iraq,
looks older next to young boys
who never held a razor to their pubescent faces,
writes 126 aloud, the number of people he killed,
wishes he could erase the faces of children as he learns
to become a father once again.

They leave in silence
intimidated by the syllabus,
amazed at the price of textbooks,
determined to return the next day.

PLATANO MADURO DREAMS

Interrupted by Yankee Stadium lights
The Bronx sky
normally black like onyx
appeared smoky as it hung over
Martha, Zoila, and their stoop.

Zoila attempted to lower the volume
of her brother's 1986 boombox,
but Martha's hand protested
with a swift slap like her mother's chancleta.
La Mega was in the middle of a bachata marathon
and no one gets in the way of Martha's bachata.

Martha started in her beauty pageant voice.
Taller than her with heels.
Cannot be a Mets fan.
Trigueño. She could not see herself with a blanquito.
A lover of salsa-merengue-garifuna-and-everything-in-between.
Raises his hand in class. Volunteers at the youth center
    on the weekends.
Because he does not want to end up like his tweaker sister.
He would love Martha and only her
not like her Tío Octavio who had a family
in the States and the island.
He worked three jobs, sent money every week,
visited every other month.
His reason: he had a love to go around.
Her Tía's reason: he's a sucio who listened to too much
Lou Rawls and Barry White in the '70s.
No sucios for me!
No sucios for me!
No sucios for me!
Martha screamed to the fire escapes.
Three times so the santos can hear.

Maybe lose weight so the guys
can stop grabbing her ass
walking down crowded bodega aisles.
Touching her head
she muttered she would keep her dreads.
No weave for me, Z.
¿Para qué?
Así cómo yo vine en éste mundo.
Fuck Mirta de Perales
and her productos de belleza.

Zoila had her own dreams.
To finish college. Maybe get a PhD.
Doctor Zoila Lucia Vazquez de Jesus.
rolled right off the tongue
better than the non-existent double r's
she had a hard time saying.
Her friends including her first boyfriend
called her defective.
Her older brothers convinced she was adopted.

Timbales never beckoned Zoila's hips, feet, and shoulders.
Her body never curved liked her Cousin Xiomara's.
She wanted to be fearless like her grandmother
who squished bugs with her bare feet.
Legend has it she grabbed a descending spider in mid-air
and slammed a broomstick to the back of a mouse's head
all at the same time.

Make enough money to buy Mamí
a house with two floors.
She always wanted to say
"I'm going upstairs to lie down"
like they do in the telenovelas.

A car alarm goes off two blocks over,
and the melody of a Mr. Softee truck singing with
the bell of a coquito pushcart reminds them
that summer isn't over just yet.

STATISTIC

Frailty thy name is woman.
The Latina Ophelia
without a Hamlet
to adore her femininities,
fall on her feet and immortalize her in madness.
Instead, an infant looks at her eyes
for answers yet known.

Statistics dictate her a failure.
Job instead of a career.
Food stamps instead of perfectly clipped suburban coupons.
Section 8 housing instead of a white picket fence
and a garden filled with her favorite flowers,
(Stargazers in case anyone wondered).

When journalists and social workers
recite percentages and predictions,
she shows them mercy.
Smiling through precious Mondays
humming her daughter's favorite nursery rhyme.

ODE TO DOORKNOCKERS

for Ivelisse Rodriguez

They dangle like the chandeliers in Versailles
14 carat gold markers of 1990s fashion,
named after the noise of welcome.

Some round, some in symmetrical shapes
with her name etched in the middle
in case you forget who is turning you down.

They accompanied her through
the isolation of boarding school, New England winters,
all-nighters of higher education.

She packed them when she ran away from the world,
finding solace in the waves of Virginia Beach,
Offered them to Yemayá as she prayed over the Pacific Ocean,
tucked them in her suit pocket at job interviews
or reading Faulkner in dusty library crevices.

Threw them at suitors begging for her affections,
wore them proud on graduation days.
Her necessities for existential crises and reality checks and
the heirlooms to a fictitious daughter.

YES

Is it true that my womb
will never feel the soft pushes of an infant's feet?

Is it true my femininity has been severed
for population control?

Is it true the pill my comadre took this morning
will cause cysts to grow in her ovaries like magnolias in May?

Is it true that Atabey weeps in a petroglyph
like la Virgen
like a mother on wedding days
like a child's first seconds in this world.

.

PALMS UP

for the city of New Orleans, July 2010

Palms up New Orleans.
Relax your fists
and let the gulf run
through the crevices of your fingers.

Palms up New Orleans.
Abandoned for dead more than once
you add more life lines
as the words spill and natural disaster
compound when there's nothing natural about
poverty, murder, suicides,
homelessness, blackened waters.

Palms up New Orleans.
Because your history of resiliency
forecasts your future.

Palms up New Orleans.
Put them together
and let us pray.

THE POET'S BOMBA

The villagers dressed in white
gather around him
thanking Ashanti for his return.

Laina sings,
Llego, llego. Por fin llego.

And he did arrive. To his island.
His muse. His constant lover
Never abandoning him.
Only opening her arms wider
to comfort his soul,
listening to his muffled midnight cries
he cannot control.

And the chorus responds.
Bedigaló. Gracias por él. Bendigaló.

Bless his words that inspire the resolve to wars,
unravel distortions of truths, document the silenced.
Bless his charity for others and forgetfulness of himself.

He succumbs to the drums and cuá
his arms rise, eyes close slowly,
meditating in the energy,
ensconced in an effortless rhythm.

Llego, llego. Por fin llego.

HAIL MARIA

for María Virginia Garcia Lozada

Because when your baby brother knocked on your door
you promoted yourself from aunt to mother without hesitation
and when cancer took your sister's left breast
you set the table for three more children.

Hail María,
because when a ring was put on your finger you declined,
you already had responsibilities in the name of
Carmen, Diana, Norma, José, y Melba
and when an unexpected grandchild was placed on your lap
you made sure she was loved.

Hail María,
Because when your mother lost her independence
you washed her body every night
and even though your womb never felt the pain of birth
your heart felt the anguish of a parent.

Hail María,
because when you were born
you lived up to the prophecy of your name.

PEDRO'S BODEGA

The 9th grade was too hard for him
so he left and moved to Nueva York.
$50 one-way airline tickets
made him special.
No boat, bus, or train for him and his dream.

He flew back and forth
over the oxidized icon of freedom,
her seven-point crown, broken shackled feet, and
the Emma Lazarus poem he could not read.

The first bodega opened
in the South Bronx on St. Ann's.
Home of quarter water, Malta, Budweiser,
and banana flavored Now and Later.
In the '90s, he moved her to Parkchester
one block from Ortiz funeral home and the 6 train.

Across the street a beat up door with no address
masked as the headquarters for a numbers game.
10 year old children ran back and forth
with a bet, a twenty and strict instructions from their mothers
to come back with a receipt and luck.

Young vets who missed the Vietnam War by that much
hung outside until 1 a.m.
Held their own ice cold interpretations
of a brown bag lunch.
Talked trash about each other's beer bellies,
thinning hair, dead end jobs, old ladies.
Collectively paused to admire The Valdez's sisters
in their high school uniforms
buy groceries for their family.

At 3 p.m. anxious children bombarded the arcade
like ants on cotton candy
waiting to see who would beat
the latest top scorer in Centipede.
Feeding games with quarters
and their stomachs with pork rinds.
White joysticks covered in the residue
of nuclear orange process cheese powder.

Women with blue hair and dark moles
with the one piece of hair on it
gossiped about Don Felix's hand
getting cut on the deli slicer.

The chisme began with 30 stitches but
by closing when Pedro let the iron gate
touched down on the broken cement
Don Felix's hand had to be amputated.

THANK YOU RICKY MARTIN

For shaking your bon-bon in 1999
bringing Grammy audiences to their feet,
giving birth to terms like The Latin Boom,
The Latin Invasion, and crossover sensation.

My Menudo T-shirt was fashionable again,
along with leather pants, blond highlights, and Boricua red lip-
stick.
Rolling my r's was sexy,
my bubble butt admired by girls with ironing board for asses,
guys asked to be called papi.

Music thanks you Rick Martín
demanding more trumpets, congas, timbales, güiros,
as part of their symphonies.

And dance followed like a lover,
as legs stretched backwards and forwards,
shoulders swayed left, right, left, right,
hips circled, pelvises gyrated like Elvis on Ed Sullivan.
Bodies sweated vertically
with a horizontal sensuality.

Spanish surnames became relevant,
names with accents and the squiggly thing
above an "n" were cool looking because
human resources need more cool around the office.

Because of you Ricky Martín,
Jennifer begot JLo, Shakira dyed her hair blonde,
Beyonce sang in Spanish, Big Pun shattered the stereotype
    of the Latin Lover,
and The Latin Grammys graduated to its own night versus
    a category.

Magazine covers looked more exotic,
while tanning salons popped up like Starbucks.
Looking orange like a kumquat was the new little black dress.
Casting calls searched for the next Latino Brad Pitt
on César Chávez Avenue, Tito Puente Way, and Humboldt Park.

Thank you Ricky Martín for making
capitalism realize the power of our wallets,
politicians recognize us as a voting bloc,
scholars dub us a walking paradox as the largest minority.

Five months after your ovation and kisses from Madonna,
Newsweek discovered us like a conquistador,
with intellectual articles titled
"The Legacy of Generation Ñ" and
"Latino America: Hispanics are hip, hot, and making history."

Mothers thank you Ricky Martín because
Guillermos who wanted to be called Bill
became Guillermos once again and
susurrus ancestors
rose from abandoned graves.

Thank you Ricky Martín.
Gracias.

LETTERS TO A YOUNG LATINA POET

I

Dear Y.L.P.
Even Rilke forgot a few things mujer.
Don't be afraid to write about your languages,
the one you were born with,
the one you had to learn
to survive, eat, explain your last name,
and the language you created.
Accents and ñ's are the adobo of a poem.
Remember what Pietri said,
"the masses are asses" and
you are not writing for them.

Go ahead
write about
your mom and grandma
washing underwear in the bathroom sink
hanging panties on the shower proudly
like spoils of war.
Scrubbing manchas out
with the flesh of their knuckles
remembering all of their guerras
and the ones you too will face.

Never be shy about underwear.
Never.

II

Querida Y.L.P.
What is this I hear about being ashamed of
your Saturday night rituals?

Watching Sábado Gigante
with abuela and abuelo
as they wait to see El Chacal
and the lucky winner of this week's car.

Not everyone will understand
but that's ok.
They will become fans of Don Francisco
and his perfectly coiffed pompadour.

Please finish writing your Walter Mercado poem
and the intense way
your Tía Lourdes listens when
he gets to Sagittarius.
He will be right one year.

Abrazos fuerte.

III

Hola Y.L.P.
¿Cómo te va?
I hope you are recovering from the flu
which reminds me I need to visit the Botanica
and stock up on my winter supply of
Vicks Vaporub and agua de Florida.
Thanks to my great-grandmother's wisdom
I know that a combination of those two
on my chest and feet
with an egg under my bed
takes away my cold just like that.

Your last letter asked what to do with family poems.
Not the ones about Christmas and quinceñeras.
But the ones about the cousin who didn't
know his boundaries, the 18 year-old half-sister
welcoming her second abortion, the graduation party

gone awry due to Tío Papo's love affair with
Johnny Caminando.

Write them querida.
Let go of the shame and the fear.
Document every slap to the face,
every hija desagradecida and "no, please no."
Read them aloud to yourself,
at open mics, or at the
new independent bookstore.

Con mucho cariño.

IV

Feliz Navidad Y.L.P.
Christmas is almost here
which means New Year's will be sooner.
Another year of resolutions
that I hope to keep.

What about you?
Do you have any new resolutions
or are you like me and extend the deadline
to the ones you made last year?
I read your love poem.
You chose a sonnet.
I can see you've been reading
Neruda and perhaps a little
bit of Parker.

Did he really break up over email?
Is that what happens when people meet online?
Everything happens over the Internet.
Connections. Dating. Sex. Breakups.
Makeup chat sex. Then the infamous
email/Facebook/MySpace/Twitter block.

I am sorry comadre.
You deserve better but
if it is any consolation
your use of simile when comparing
his penis to the size of a baby carrot
was perfection.

Abrazos.

V

Mi comadre Y.L.P.
I am sorry for the lag between letters
but life has been difficult.
My poor abuelita poems were rejected yet again.
Who rejects granny?
Insensitive orphaned editors that's who.
But forget them and their
"We are sorry to inform you" form letters.

I will take my abuelita poems elsewhere.
How she taught me to
hem my own skirt, sew buttons,
knit blankets and matching booties
for expectant mothers and their infants.
Cook pasteles for the entire block,
leave some in the freezer for widows
who forget to eat while mourning their señors.

Oddly enough, they liked my ménage à trois poem.
You know the one with me and two other men
who instead of making me orgasm
one cleans my house, washes my dishes,
changes the oil to my car, fixes the leaky bathroom faucet,
while the other massages my feet
then paints my toes
cotton candy pink
all without complaining.

Next letter I will address your
issues with aesthetics and form.
Sestinas are fun but
iambic pentameter is the devil.

Besitos.

VI

My Y.L.P.
Learn from my mistakes and
don't email the editor who rejected you and
call him a *hijo de gran puta*.
Who knew he spent a year abroad in Santo Domingo?

By the way,
this is my last letter for a while.
I was accepted to a residency program
where I will eat, sleep, and speak revision.
Isolated from distractions like Farmville,
dying my hair blond one more time, or
2 a.m. rendezvous with ex-boyfriends
wondering why they got married.
I think I will be somewhere in New England.
These residencies are always in New England.

Hasta la próxima.

ABOUT THE AUTHOR

Luivette Resto *was born in Aguas Buenas, Puerto Rico but proudly raised in the Bronx. Her first book of poetry,* Unfinished Portrait, *was published in 2008 by Tía Chucha Press and later named a finalist for the 2009 Paterson Poetry Prize. She is a contributing poetry editor for* Kweli Journal, *a CantoMundo fellow, and the hostess of a monthly poetry reading series called* La Palabra *located at Avenue 50 Studio in Los Angeles.*